BIGGEST NAMES IN MUSIC
ARIANA GRANDE

by Martha London

FOCUS
READERS®

NAVIGATOR

WWW.FOCUSREADERS.COM

Focus Readers is distributed by North Star Editions:
sales@northstareditions.com | 888-417-0195

Produced for Focus Readers by Red Line Editorial.

Photographs ©: Ryan Phillips/PA Wire URN:33206724/Press Association/AP Images, cover, 1; Lucas Jackson/Reuters/Newscom, 4–5; Noam Galai/WireImage/Getty Images, 7; Shutterstock Images, 8–9, 13, 20–21, 29; Walter McBride/Corbis Entertainment/Getty Images, 11; Alex J. Berliner/AP Images, 14–15; Charles Sykes/Invision/AP Images, 17; John Shearer/Invision/AP Images, 19, 24; Matt Sayles/Invision/AP Images, 22; Alex Brandon/AP Images, 27

Library of Congress Cataloging-in-Publication Data
Names: London, Martha, author.
Title: Ariana Grande / by Martha London.
Description: Lake Elmo, MN : Focus Readers, 2021. | Series: Biggest names in music | Includes index. | Audience: Grades 4-6
Identifiers: LCCN 2020011101 (print) | LCCN 2020011102 (ebook) | ISBN 9781644936344 (hardcover) | ISBN 9781644936436 (paperback) | ISBN 9781644936610 (pdf) | ISBN 9781644936528 (ebook)
Subjects: LCSH: Grande, Ariana--Juvenile literature. | Singers--United States--Biography--Juvenile literature.
Classification: LCC ML3930.G724 L66 2021 (print) | LCC ML3930.G724 (ebook) | DDC 782.42164092 [B]--dc23
LC record available at https://lccn.loc.gov/2020011101
LC ebook record available at https://lccn.loc.gov/2020011102

Printed in the United States of America
Mankato, MN
082020

ABOUT THE AUTHOR

Martha London writes books for young readers full-time. She enjoys all types of music. In high school and college, she spent several years performing in musicals.

TABLE OF CONTENTS

CHAPTER 1

A TEAM OF WOMEN

Tall columns rose high above the stage at the 2018 MTV Video Music Awards (VMAs). Ariana Grande was about to perform. She had been **nominated** for five awards, including Best Pop Video and Artist of the Year.

Fifty women took their places at a long table onstage. Grande sat in the middle.

Ariana Grande (center) performs during the 2018 MTV VMAs.

As she began to sing, the women started dancing. Grande was performing "God Is a Woman." The song's words were **empowering** to women.

The dancers moved smoothly across the stage. Many wore colorful costumes that sparkled. The crowd cheered as Grande began singing the **refrain**. It was time for her to show off her signature vocal skills. Her powerful voice rose to hit a series of very high notes.

At the end of the song, Grande pulled three people to the front of the stage. They were her mother, cousin, and grandmother. The four women bowed. The audience stood and cheered. People

Grande's cousin (left), grandmother (center), and mother (right) have all had important roles in her life.

were moved by Grande's choice to include her family onstage. Like her song, this choice celebrated women's impact and importance.

CHAPTER 2

GROWING UP ONSTAGE

Ariana Grande was born in Boca Raton, Florida, on June 26, 1993. She began singing and performing when she was very young.

In 2003, Ariana's parents divorced. Ariana was only 10 years old. Her mother raised her and her half brother, Frankie. Ariana didn't see her father very often.

Ariana and Frankie Grande attend the MTV Movie Awards together in 2013.

But she says she had a good childhood. Her mom encouraged her to follow her dreams.

Ariana began performing in her community theater. She enjoyed being onstage. Audiences noticed her talent right away. Ariana continued to **audition**

LEARNING FROM THE MASTERS

Ariana grew up in a musical home. Her family had a karaoke machine. Ariana sang along to songs by Judy Garland, Céline Dion, Madonna, and Whitney Houston. Singing along with these talented women taught Ariana how to use her voice. She tried to sing the way they sang. She learned how to sing without hurting her voice.

Ariana performs as Charlotte in the Broadway musical *13*.

for more shows. In 2006, she got her big break. She tried out for a Broadway musical called *13*. She got the part of Charlotte. The musical opened in New York in 2008. Ariana was 14 years old.

Ariana had a small part in the musical. But she was featured in a couple of the musical's songs. Audience members and **critics** saw her talent. They praised her singing ability.

The show closed in 2009. Ariana enjoyed acting. But she wanted to be a singer. She searched for a studio where she could begin recording. However, her **manager** told her that she shouldn't start recording albums yet. She should build her career on TV first.

Ariana followed her manager's advice. She landed a role on the Nickelodeon TV show *Victorious*. She played Cat, who was cheerful but not very smart.

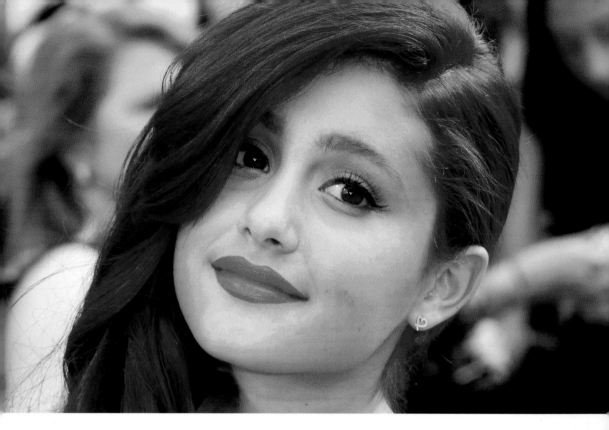

Ariana dyed her hair red while playing Cat Valentine.

When *Victorious* ended in 2012, Ariana wanted to start making music. Instead, she got a part in a new TV show called *Sam & Cat*. This show was based on *Victorious*. Ariana continued playing the same silly character.

CHAPTER 3

TIME TO MAKE MUSIC

Grande didn't want to spend the rest of her life acting in TV shows. She wanted to make music. But she had trouble getting record companies to pay attention to her. **Producers** only saw the silly character she played on TV. They didn't think she could be a serious singer.

Grande's singing career got its start while she was still acting.

Grande did not let that stop her. She decided to make music on her own. She performed covers of songs and uploaded them to YouTube. A cover is a song that was originally performed by another artist.

THE NEXT MARIAH CAREY?

Grande has a four-octave range. She can sing very high and very low. Few singers have such a large range. In 2012, Grande posted a cover of a Mariah Carey song on YouTube. Carey is known for singing extremely high notes. Grande hit them all perfectly. Some people began calling her the next Mariah Carey. Grande admires Carey. However, Grande wants to do more than imitate other artists. She hopes to have a musical style that is all her own.

"The Way" was one of the first singles Grande released.

In 2012, Grande posted a cover of "Die in Your Arms" by Justin Bieber. It spread across the internet. It even caught the attention of Bieber's manager, Scooter Braun. Braun was impressed.

He contacted Grande and offered her a recording **contract**. Grande accepted. She could finally start recording music.

Grande released her first album less than a year later. It was called *Yours Truly*. To reach more fans, Grande joined Bieber's tour for his latest album. She was his opening act. Grande sang her songs before he came onstage. She performed in only a few shows on that tour. But audiences and critics were impressed. Grande won Best New Artist at the American Music Awards (AMAs) in 2013.

Almost as soon as *Yours Truly* was released, Grande began recording her second album. *My Everything* came out

Grande performs at the 2013 AMAs in Los Angeles, California.

in 2014. Both of these albums opened at No. 1 on *Billboard*'s Hot 100 chart. Few artists receive such immediate success. But Grande was just getting started.

CHAPTER 4

ROCKETING TO STARDOM

Grande announced her first headlining tour in 2014. She was the star performer at each concert. The next year, she set out on an even bigger tour. She played concerts for fans around the world. By 2016, she had released a third album, *Dangerous Woman*. And in 2017, she went on another world tour.

Grande is known for her style. She often wears a high ponytail and tall boots.

Grande was named Artist of the Year at the 2016 AMAs.

People loved Grande's music. Her catchy songs often had upbeat rhythms. Fans enjoyed singing along. Grande's music also showed off her voice. She sang in many different styles, including pop and R&B.

Grande continued to challenge herself. She wanted to make music that was completely her own. So, after her second world tour, Grande returned to her studio. She recorded her fourth album, *Sweetener.* This album was released in August 2018. It had the style of music Grande had wanted to make since she was 14 years old.

Grande sang about her **anxiety**. She also sang about love. The songs were emotional. But they were also fun to dance to. Fans loved the album. Critics praised it as well. They said it showed a distinct style. Her song "No Tears Left to Cry" won Best Pop Video at the VMAs.

Grande performs at the 57th Grammy Awards ceremony in 2015.

And *Sweetener* won Best Pop Vocal Album at the 61st Grammy Awards.

Grande's next album was even more personal. She recorded *Thank U, Next* in just a few weeks. Many people called it one of her best albums. At one point, singles from the album had the top three spots on *Billboard*'s Hot 100. Getting the top three spots on this chart at the same time is very rare. The last group to do so was the Beatles in 1964.

Grande says she feels humbled by her success. She knows she is lucky. She loves her fans and tries to support them the way they support her. She also wants to use her fame to make positive change.

For example, Grande wants to help dogs in animal shelters. She encourages people to adopt them. In 2015, she brought puppies with her on her world tour. Fans could adopt the dogs for free.

By the end of the tour, all of the dogs she sponsored had been adopted.

In 2018, Grande performed at the March for Our Lives protest. The protest occurred after a school shooting in

ATTACK IN MANCHESTER

Grande's 2017 tour included a concert in Manchester, England. As the show was ending, a man set off a bomb. It killed 23 people. Grande was shocked. She began making plans to help the victims and their families. Grande returned to Manchester two weeks later. She visited people affected by the attack. And she put on a concert to raise money to help the community recover. Several famous musicians joined her. Together, they raised $25 million.

Grande sings "Be Alright" at the March for Our Lives protest in Washington, DC.

Florida. It was led by students who wanted to end gun violence. Grande's performance helped raise money to support victims of the attack. Since then, Grande has continued to speak up for causes she believes in. She inspires her fans to make change, too.

ARIANA GRANDE

- Birth date: June 26, 1993
- Birthplace: Boca Raton, Florida
- Family members: Joan (mother), Edward (father), Frankie (half brother)
- High school: North Broward Preparatory School
- Major accomplishments:
  - January 2008: Grande begins acting in the Broadway musical *13*.
  - March 2010: Grande starts playing Cat Valentine in the Nickelodeon show *Victorious*.
  - July 2012: Grande's cover of "Die in Your Arms" helps her get a recording contract.
  - September 2013: Grande's first album, *Yours Truly*, debuts at No. 1.
  - February 2019: *Sweetener* wins a Grammy for Best Pop Vocal Album.

Grande performs in Philadelphia, Pennsylvania, in 2014.

- Quote: "I'm a huge advocate of self-expression, being yourself, and encouraging people to embrace who they are and the things that make them beautiful. I love people's uniqueness— the quirky, weird, interesting, and different things about everybody."

Sarah Kinonen. "Ariana Grande Opens Up About Self-Expression and Loving Her Fans." *Allure*. Condé Nast, 6 Oct. 2017. Web. 25 Feb. 2020.

FOCUS ON
ARIANA GRANDE

Write your answers on a separate piece of paper.

1. Write a paragraph summarizing the main ideas of Chapter 2.

2. Would you rather be an actor on a TV show or a musician in a band? Why?

3. Which album's singles gave Grande the top three spots on *Billboard*'s Hot 100?
   - **A.** *Dangerous Woman*
   - **B.** *My Everything*
   - **C.** *Thank U, Next*

4. What might have happened if Grande hadn't uploaded her music to YouTube?
   - **A.** It might have taken longer for her to get a recording contract.
   - **B.** She might have gotten a recording contract more quickly.
   - **C.** She might have made more money from her songs.

Answer key on page 32.

GLOSSARY

anxiety
A feeling of extreme worry or nervousness.

audition
To try out for a part in a play or musical group.

contract
An agreement that a musician makes to work with a specific recording company.

critics
People who review music and give their thoughts on it.

empowering
Encouraging people to feel like they can do something.

manager
A person who works with performers to help them plan their careers.

nominated
Chosen as a finalist for an award or honor.

producers
People who work with musicians to record songs.

refrain
A repeated section of a song.

TO LEARN MORE

BOOKS

Baxter, Roberta. *Women in Music*. Minneapolis: Abdo Publishing, 2019.

Santos, Rita. *Ariana Grande: Pop Star*. New York: Enslow Publishing, 2019.

Schwartz, Heather E. *Ariana Grande: Music Superstar*. Minneapolis: Lerner Publications, 2020.

NOTE TO EDUCATORS

Visit **www.focusreaders.com** to find lesson plans, activities, links, and other resources related to this title.

INDEX

Answer Key: 1. Answers will vary; **2.** Answers will vary; **3.** C; **4.** A